Heidi Jo

by Robert Shunk

DORRANCE PUBLISHING CO
EST. 1920
PITTSBURGH, PENNSYLVANIA 15238

Dorrance Publishing Co
585 Alpha Drive
Pittsburgh, PA 15238
Visit our website at *www.dorrancebookstore.com*

ISBN: 979-8-88925-005-0
eISBN: 979-8-88925-505-5

Heidi Jo

An Irish family, long ago,
From o'er across the sea,
Set sail to find a life anew—
They yearned for liberty.

Oh, bless their hearts, we welcomed them,
When they came to our shore
And joy, it was, to have them here,
To share their hearts and more.

Their hearts were full of love and hope,
Excitement filled their eyes.
They sparkled, like the Irish do,
In sunlit morning skies.

The will they had was strong and kind,
Toward all, their lives would share.
They were a gift to this new land—
Our Nation's heart would care.

I saw their never—ending toil—
The hours they worked were long.
But not one word did they complain;
They always had a song.

A melody was in their hearts,
To help along life's road.
Their children worked right by their side,
To help them bear the load.

They set out working every day—
The sunset gave them rest,
Their hearts determined on a life
Of freedom at its best.

They wanted naught but to be free
And raise their children good.
God gave to them a land of love,
The Irish understood.

The family stood so strong in faith.
Our God was always there
Through days of pain and nights of tears—
When no one else would care.

Through sickness, death, and time of mourn,
This family just wouldn't quit.
It must have been the USA
That prided them a bit.

This Irish bloodline would not stop,
It carried many years.
The children grew, their children, too,
And none were without tears.

The tears were oft', the suffering, sure,
But they continued on,
For in their hearts, great freedom held
A future not forlorn.

God sent this Irish family here,
So very long ago,
And knew one day a child would come,
Whose name was Heidi Jo.

Now Heidi Jo would grow, in time,
A pretty little lass—
And in her heart she'd hold the joy
of moments that would pass.

God placed within her tender heart,
A smile, so soft and warm,
But God gave something special, too,
When Heidi Jo was born...

He gave this world a touch of light
That ne'er so shined before,
It shines so bright within the soul,
Of one I so adore.

The tiers of times of Heidi Jo,
Both joy and sadness share—
They hold the hills and valleys, too:
They tell of one so rare.

One tier holds a burst of joy,
Another holds a fear—
"Tis quite a struggle for her heart—
This soul, I love so dear.

I look from naught, through her green eyes,
I see her soul within
Deep down, I see the hopes and dreams
She struggles there to win.

I see, I feel, her toil deep down.
I see her pain in sight,
But who am I, that God would call
For missions in the night?

Now, up one hill and down again,
Then, to the valley low—
So goes the life of Heidi Jo,
But, who could ever know?

A special lass, my Heidi Jo,
A special heart inside:
A humble spirit gives to her
A tone of certain pride.

But not that pride of selfishness,
She's not the one to boast—
But, pride in Him who loves us all—
That greatest King of Host.

I know her life would show less pain
If only she could know
The full extent of God's great love,
That keeps her smiling so.

I pray to God, each day I breathe,
To keep my Heidi Jo,
And bring her forth, from paths of sin
That her own heart, to know.

Lord, break Your silence from above—
She needs You, don't You know?
Come, whisper to the lonely heart
Of my sweet, Heidi Jo.

And Lord, I pray, if it's Thy will,
Set forth Thy moral code
Within the boundary of her heart,
And lift the unpure load.

But, if its fate, she bear this load—
This burden, oh, so great,
Then give her strength, Lord God, I pray
To help her bear the weight.

And if she starts to slip or fall
Upon life's rocky road,
Don't cast more stones before her feet,
Just help her bear the load.

The secret windows of her soul
Reveal to me, in part,
Abundant love, so full of hope—
It overwhelms my heart.

I have not e'er so much as dreamed
Of one so preciously.
The beauty of her spirit sings
To me abundantly.

Oh, beauty spirit, bright and pure,
Have victory in your soul.
Don't succumb to wickedness,
And pay that terrible toll.

I see the precious tier of hope
That nestles Heidi Jo,
So snug and warm, beneath God's shield,
To keep her heart aglow.

A pillar in her life stands small,
But has much room to grow.
God, send Thy gift of food for soul
I pray, for Heidi Jo.

Taste in thy soul of righteousness,
I beg you, Heidi Jo.
And use this tier of hope within
To make this pillar grow.

Put lust aside and turn away,
Be humble, Heidi Jo.
Look up to our eternal God,
You'll have less toil and woe.

No matter what the day may bring,
Just clouds or rain of tears—
The smile upon her face is clear,
She tries to hide her fears.

But I can see the trouble there,
Beyond that smile, just so,
God lets me visit down within
The soul of Heidi Jo.

And what I see, brings tears and prayer—
I know God hears me pray.
In my own heart, I suffer, too,
When Heidi Jo's astray.

Oh, Lord, my God, protect this lass
And save her humble heart—
We cannot cease in prayer or deeds,
And let her life depart.

I see so much within her, deep,
It's hard to tell of all—
For Heidi Jo, it's been some toil,
From younger days, recall.

I saw a tier of suffering there
Beneath her beaming eyes.
I felt the pain of Heidi Jo,
I heard her troubled cries.

One tier of suffering stood alone.
And made me well aware
Of so much hurt and bitter pain—
I shed a tear, with care.

The tier unfolded, like a scroll
To show her life, in past—
It held me there, just like a weight,
To make the vision last.

I saw the tier of time that put
My Heidi Jo in pain—
I tremble when I think about
That crash, just down the lane.

The feel of splendor, on that ride,
On one fine summer day,
So quickly turned to fear and hurt,
And brushed the joy away.

So young and sweet and full of joy—
A heart so free and pure.
Her smile, most present all the time,
But soon, would be no more.

A sudden slip—A twisted turn—
Her flesh was torn apart—
God must have put her through this trial,
To stronger make her heart.

I see her fall—I feel her pain—
I see her tears of shock.
I hear her stinging, suffering screams,
But I can't turn the clock.

Now, as she suffers there, alone,
With no help near, in sight,
I want to be back there in time
To help her win this fight.

God surely must have been there, too,
Beside my Heidi Jo.
Although, it's hard to understand
Just why she suffered so.

But who could know what waits for one
Just down a lane of terror?
God has not promised one more day,
Nor one more breath of air.

Now Heidi Jo, with broken flesh
Defies the march of death.
Although she suffers fearfully,
God does not take her breath.

I saw an angel sit with her,
Throughout this painful time—
I saw the angel comfort her
And sing to her in rhyme.

The angel softly stroked her hair
and held her tender hand.
It looked as though, this gift from God,
Was fully in command.

Through days and nights, this angel sat,
And wiped her tears away.
A much persistent one of God,
Who didn't wear out its stay.

As one tear flowed, another dropped,
But even warriors cry,
And Heidi Jo was so much more
This warrior would not die.

Each day that passed seemed like a week—
This splendid girl hung on.
It had to be the will of God,
Her heart was not forlorn.

A flood of tears and then a smile
Upon her battered face,
Let my heart know that Heidi Jo
Would make it with God's grace.

Now, Heidi Jo would mend in time—
God healed this dear, sweet girl,
Then stayed to mold her heart within—
More precious than a pearl.

Although her face may show the scars,
Of battles years ago,
The sunshine from her pleasant smile,
Puts all her face aglow.

Now, one great storm has passed her life—
A giant storm, you know
It must have been the hand of God
That healed my Heidi Jo.

She's learned to cope with troubled times—
God strengthened her own will,
And stood her precious heart, so bright—
My heart; her smiles fulfill.

She's quite a wonder of the years—
A beauty born in peace,
And set upon the path of life,
Whose smiles just never cease.

God must have searched the stars above
To find her nice, bright smile.
And placed it there upon her face,
To make this charming gal.

Oh, what a splendid piece of joy
To see her smile, so bright—
I feel her presence always near—
She's like a ray of light.

Oh, what a precious gift from God—
The smile of Heidi Jo.
She's one to cherish for all time—
Her inspirations flow.

I thank my God above each day
For sending her my way,
And giving her a heart of gold,
That shines with soft array.

I will not e'er, in time, forget
My lovely Heidi Jo,
Nor will I e'er forget, in time,
Her smile, so much aglow.

Through her bright eyes, I travel paths
My soul could only go.
What awesome tiers of time, I see,
Inside of Heidi Jo.

The sparkle of her gifted eyes
And her inspiring smile,
Could light the darkest path at night
And split a maple bough.

She shares a portion of great love—
The love of God on high.
Oh, somewhere deep within this lass,
There dwells a sunny sky.

Not far from many other tiers,
I see a tier of light.
I linger there, in purest awe,
To search this mass, so bright.

The source of light came from her heart,
And outward, it did flow.
My human mind could not absorb
This tier in Heidi Jo.

I could not fully understand
The purpose of this tier,
But it most surely gave to her
A burst of God's own cheer.

A massive light! A beauty light!
Transparent from each side.
It's very hard to comprehend,
It acts most like a tide.

It pulsates in, then, back again—
It has a blinding glow.
It so appears it wants to gain
Some space in Heidi Jo.

The light attempts to enter in
The corridors of her life,
But faces some rejection there,
From darkness, full of strife.

The light retreats, to try again,
Insistent upon a gain—
Oh, Heidi Jo, please let this light
Flow o'er your soul of pain—

Into your heart, into your mind
And to your very thought—
Please, Heidi Jo, accept this gift,
Before your life is naught.

So many tiers, within the life
Of pretty Heidi Jo—
Some tiers, I just can't talk about,
They dwell, to hurt me so.

How precious is my Heidi Jo.
How faithful is her heart.
How tender are her thoughts within—
I pray, will not depart.

The humble heart of Heidi Jo
Is always open wide;
To hear, to talk, to listen well—
In her, I can confide.

There is a certain peace with her.
I envy it so much.
I'd love to have this peace within,
To share, to hold, to touch.

I saw a tier of deep respect,
Within my Heidi Jo,
But it was covered o'er in time,
By pretense, on the go.

Deceit put lust across this tier
And soaked it to the core.
It holds the heart of Heidi Jo
In bondage, like a lure.

I pray to God above each day,
To save my Heidi Jo
From sinking into sin of lust,
To suffer far below.

If God could read my many tears,
From my own heart, they flow;
He'd have a thousand books to read
About my Heidi Jo.

I ponder o'er those lovely tiers:
The tiers of all her time—
The precious life, within her soul,
Is wasted in her prime.

How gently can I tell her heart,
How tender can I say:
"God loves you, Heidi Jo, so much,
He sent me by your way—

To talk with you, to pray for you,
Steadfastly, in the truth,
To help you find a better way
To mend your body's youth.

I need to tell you Heidi Jo,
You're walking in the sand,
You'll surely sink, if you don't turn—
I pray you'll understand.

I hope the gentle whisper of
God's voice, will touch your heart
And let you feel deep in your soul,
And know my humble part.

My words will not forsake your life—
I'll never be untrue.
As sure as God is in my heart,
I'll always pray for you.

And when I get the chance to go,
I'll visit in your soul,
To see if all your tiers of time
Have reached their special goal.

One thing would please me very much,
If ever we could go,
And hand in hand, walk through the tiers
Of my sweet Heidi Jo.

Together there, within the depths
of your own heart and mind,
We both could linger o'er the joys
Deep in your soul, we'd find.

I know that tier of joy is there,
I've seen it many times,
Within your eyes, within your heart—
It rings like silver chimes.

Don't e'er despair, sweet Heidi Jo,
And don't you dare give up.
God's close enough to you to care
And help you drink your cup.

And I'll be right there, for you too,
If you allow it so.
Please let me linger in your soul,
Oh, precious Heidi Jo."

This tier of joy, I long so much,
To visit with once more,
And soak my heart with all the warmth
That flows with much adore.

The overflow of joy divine,
So quickly fades away.
It seems to me, of such a waste,
Within this mold of clay.

But, when the tier of joy runs o'er—
The cup, at present, full,
Then pleasant is the heart within.
My Heidi Jo to rule.

This tier of ever—present joy
Will quickly overflow,
To witness to all human kind
The joy of Heidi Jo.

I know one day we'll leave this life—
Both Heidi Jo and I—
And enter our eternal home,
Forever, o'er the sky.

And, there, I'll understand much more,
As Jesus lets me know,
The meaning of my visits to
The tiers of Heidi Jo.

But, as my God lets me go on,
To tarry here below,
As long as I shall live in time,
I'll cherish Heidi Jo.

And hold her soul so close to me
With all those tiers inside—
To feel that goodness in her heart
That gives me humble pride.

What is this pride within me deep?
What is this joy I feel?
Is it the soul of Heidi Jo,
So close, my heart would kneel?

To beg her hand—her tender hand
And hold her close to me,
Then whisper to her, words of hope,
That float so tenderly...

Across her heart, so free and pure
And deep within her grace;
To make that precious smile of hers,
Shine bright upon her face.

I feel her smile that splendid smile—
Just right inside of me,
No matter where the day may lead,
It's with me constantly.

I want to tell of faith, I've seen
While on a trek, so deep—
The tier of faith in Heidi Jo
Caused me to stop and weep.

This tier of faith, I wept so for,
Needs prayer for it to grow.
It's waiting there so patiently,
This tier in Heidi Jo.

I saw the space around this tier,
So empty and forlorn,
It wants to grow, to fill her soul,
But Heidi Jo walks on.

I pray that she will stop awhile—
A moment to reflect
And ponder o'er this tier of faith,
To give it all respect.

I humbly bow before this tier,
And pray to God above,
For faith to grow in Heidi Jo
And in this soul we love.

My heart will pray each night and day,
For faith to multiply,
Within the boundary of this tier
And stronger grow it, nigh.

Lord, touch this tier, in this sweet life,
Of one we love so dear,
And make a faithful pillar there,
So strong, and yet, so near.

And let the faith be strong enough
To well equip her heart,
With righteousness so full of joy,
It will not e'er depart.

Throughout my time upon this earth,
I'll yearn to visit oft,
The tiers within this precious soul,
That light her heart, so soft.

The tier of softness, glowing there,
That flowed from midst her heart,
Was quite an awesome sight to see—
The gentle waves ne'er part.

The tier of softness gives to her,
A kind and tender smile,
That glows so bright within her eyes,
Like lightning on the prowl.

A perfect fit upon her face,
Just like her heart inside,
Consuming those who look upon
Her life, so well applied.

God made this life of Heidi Jo
So special on this earth.
He sent her here from up above,
To better make our worth.

God touched her life and put within,
Some Manna for her soul,
To brighten more, the world around—
In secret, write her scroll.

Oh, tier of life, I see so bright,
Sound out your joyous call,
And let her know, you live inside,
Stand firm, supreme, and tall.

Speak to the heart of Heidi Jo
And lift her joy to height.
Oh, tier of life, don't let us lose
This precious beam of light.

She's one great smile within my heart,
A star, upon my sky,
A flaming light within my world,
Encircling me so high.

Her smile is like a flowing stream,
Of water running pure—
Most like a river in her soul—
A well, forever sure.

Shore up this tier of life, oh Lord,
Restore my Heidi Jo,
And let her smile be ever there,
To keep our world aglow.

She's so much pleasing to my heart,
So wonderful, her smile,
Oh, tier of life, don't let us lose
This water of the Nile.

What is this burning in my soul
A flame so high and fierce,
That holds my heart, my very breath,
In captive there, to pierce?

Oh, tier of joy, you take my breath
And scar my heart of love,
Inside the soul of Heidi Jo,
As gentle as a dove.

Release my heart and let me see
The fullness of this tier,
That sparkles bright in Heidi Jo,
To keep her joy so near.

I breathe so scarce, to look upon,
This tier of perfect joy,
Within the realm of Heidi Jo,
My heartbeat to destroy.

This sea of joy, that floods my soul,
The waves so crystal clear,
Within the depths of Heidi Jo,
So, bond me to this tier.

If I could tell of all the joy
About this tier I know,
That lies inside those beaming eyes—
The eyes of Heidi Jo...

You, too, would be so overwhelmed
with joy abundant, near—
Much like a gift from God's own hand,
But, dwells in one, so dear.

I cannot understand this joy,
That flows from God's own throne.
Oh, what a love, that's rooted deep—
To Heidi Jo—her own.

Just like a sailor on the sea,
But sailing waves of tears,
So is my heart, when I must tell,
About these precious tiers.

My words are anchored in a prayer,
But pulled through flooded tears
And better knows no one than I,
The toll of suffering years.

While in the soul of Heidi Jo,
My tears fell deep below,
The floor upon her soul is soaked
As heart—felt yearnings grow.

Tear drops from this heart of mine,
That pains so bad, inside,
Flow in the soul of Heidi Jo—
Compassion's on a ride.

I read the tiers of Heidi Jo
Just like a book, so long—
An open book, so full of joy,
A life just like a song.

The song unfolds continuous—
The harmony is pure.
How wonderful, this journey is
Through tiers, forever more.

A wounded tier lay grim and low
Beneath much pain, in time,
And needed some compassion there,
To help this tier to climb.

Oh, tier of great compassion there,
Reach out and touch this lass,
And heal this wound within her soul,
That all the hurt, may pass.

My very soul is overwhelmed.
My heart is moved so great.
The very touch of Heidi Jo
Makes sadness face its fate.

Her tender hand, her gentle touch,
Tells volumes, this I know,
But no words known to human kind
Could tell of Heidi Jo.

You have to feel, deep in your heart,
The words not known to man,
And keep them there, in secret place,
To fully understand.

I strive to tell how wonderful
Her spirit, pure and whole,
But all the words just echo back
And scramble to my soul.

I've seen the tears, drop from the eyes—
The eyes of Heidi Jo—
The same soft eyes I look upon
To see her spirit flow.

And in her tear drops I can see,
A humble, thankful tier—
A heart of goodness, soul of care,
Much mercy, sweet and dear.

God knows the heart of Heidi Jo.
He looks not on her past.
He will not leave her soul to grope.
Her joy will surely last.

And in her joy, I too, can share
Those tender times I see.
It's quite a trek for Heidi Jo
To give this liberty.

I see the tier of mercy, there
Inside of Heidi Jo,
This pulse of warmth and comfort great
My soul could only know.

Like winter snow in springtime sun,
Her heart melts warm and soft.
This tier of mercy makes her so;
Her radiance, aloft.

I've seen this tier of mercy work,
Its cloak so warm and kind.
Oh, truly blessed is Heidi Jo
This tier is mine to find.

I've seen this tier of mercy great
Inside of Heidi Jo,
And as it poured all out at will,
This tier began to grow.

Compassion grew so tall and bold,
I thought the tier would burst.
What mercy lies within this well—
What drink for souls of thirst!

The cup upon this tier is full
With mercy to the top,
And Heidi Jo knows how to share
The harvest of her crop.

No one, I know, has cloudless days,
Nor sky that has no rain,
Some days are meant to be that way,
And some have so much pain.

But when my Heidi Jo is near,
With her great smile, so bright,
You need not worry 'bout your day—
Your heart will have delight.

She is a gift to my sad heart,
A torch, to my life's core;
A glowing star within my soul,
A gem I can't ignore.

What is this force that tugs upon
My steady aching heart,
And begs me in to Heidi Jo,
To view her world, in part?

What are these tiers, deep in her soul
That I cannot explain?
Must I keep all them tucked away,
Within my soul to rein?

I gaze upon my Heidi Jo,
A wonder to behold!
God surely used some precious clay
To make this special mold.

God shaped this special mold of clay
And set her free at will.
'Oh, what a beauty, He hath made,
She is a wonder, still.

God placed those tiers down in her soul
And gave to Heidi Jo,
Her own sweet cup of loveliness,
For all the world to know.

The eyes of my unworthy soul,
Unworthy to behold,
But view the tiers in Heidi Jo—
Entrusted to her fold.

The tier of trust in Heidi Jo
Stood ready every day.
Now use this tier of trust, sweet lass,
And trust, but few, I pray.

Her tier of kindness, no one's felt,
Nor no one's seen, like I.
I've supped with her; she shared her cup,
And let me hold her nigh.

She shared her kindness with my heart,
I've never asked her why—
For thus, my heart already knows,
The answer for this guy.

The tier of kindness bubbles o'er
With smiles and joy galore.
They're happy bubbles, in this tier,
They sing at my life's door.

Just like a beacon on a hill,
To light the darkest night,
So is my Heidi Jo each day—
She makes a sad heart bright.

Her gentle cup of tenderness,
She freely shares with me,
And lets me see the tier inside,
That fills this cup with glee.

The tiers inside of Heidi Jo,
May take my breath away,
But such a journey's worth it all,
'Tis where I'd like to stay.

I wrap myself with waves of joy
That flow from Heidi Jo,
They mend my heart that's been so sad,
From many years ago.

I'm ever thankful to this lass,
She shared so much with me,
She shared her hopes, her dreams, her joys,
Her touch, so tenderly.

Just like a blossom in the spring
That brings forth loveliness,
So is the soul of Heidi Jo,
With beauty to caress.

This tender tier of loveliness,
That I behold with peace,
So blossoms in my Heidi Jo,
The comfort will not cease.

What is this tier, so radiant?
What is this joy, so whole?
I pray, that Heidi Jo will find
What lies in her own soul.

I pray her eyes will open soon,
That she may come to know
The very soul, that lies so deep—
The soul of Heidi Jo.

God showed a tier of radiance,
That beamed in Heidi Jo.
I saw it live with joy and hope—
Enhancement, on the go.

For all I've seen in Heidi Jo,
Would take a world to bear.
If I could have a hundred hearts,
I could not store it there.

Oh, tier of radiance, so bright,
I humbly ponder thee.
Oh, what a gift in Heidi Jo,
I hope her heart will see.

Look to your heart, sweet Heidi Jo,
And know that God is there,
Who gives you, from these tiers within,
This life you love to share.

Her smile has touched my wretched heart,
Her touch makes all hope flow,
And hope has filled my soul again,
From tiers of Heidi Jo.

My soul is filled and running o'er,
I try to catch the spill.
I simply can't absorb the joy,
 That's given me, at will.

But God retakes this over—flow
And fills the cup anew,
That I may taste of what's not lost
Of Heidi Jo's sweet brew.

What wholesome tiers, beneath the eyes,
The eyes, I've known before.
Our cups together we did share,
Our lives, our trust, and more.

I dreamed we were in Heaven above,
My Heidi Jo and I,
Were best of friends in God's great world,
That Kingdom o'er the sky.

Our fellowship was one of care,
And perfect peace within.
The perfect joy was ours to share,
Without a trace of sin.

We chose to come to earth below,
Both I and Heidi Jo,
And dress these bodies in this world
For missions our hearts know.

Now surely, Heidi Jo and I,
Called out to Heaven above,
And promised that our hearts would meet,
To share on earth such love.

As our covenant now fulfills us,
To touch our hearts on earth,
With memories of a life time
To our eternal birth.

The joys I shared with Heidi Jo,
Can ne'er be stricken down.
When we leave earth for our true home
I know, she'll have her crown,

For all the splendor, she's put forth,
While here on earth below;
What constant beauty flows from her,
From deep in Heidi Jo.

Inside this lass, a splendid tier,
That has a special light,
A light not known to human eyes,
It's just a soul's delight.

What lights this tier of splendor so,
With beauty all about?
It must be love from God's own heart,
Without a single doubt.

There must be some way to explain,
The hues the splendid hue!
No color known to human kind,
Glow from this tier I view.

Oh, Heidi Jo, if you could know,
And view this tier within,
What splendor lives inside of you,
You have so much to win.

Look to your heart, my precious one,
And seek and you will find,
Those splendid tiers and precious joys,
That thrive in you, so kind.

Oh tier of splendor, be it known,
That yours, above the rest,
Has special space in Heidi Jo,
To help her be her best.

The hues of beauty, in the soul
of Heidi Jo I view,
I cannot weep, I cannot speak—
The splendor of the hue!

Now, Heidi Jo can use this tier,
So splendid, where it lies,
To give her smiles an extra light
That beams from her bright eyes.

The utter glory of this tier,
Reveals to me so true,
That God's own hand is in her life,
To help her struggle through.

How precious is her tender hand,
That speaks to me, inside,
So many words without a sound,
So gently by my side.

The hand of God is ever near
My tender Heidi Jo.
I hope she knows how close God is,
How angels watch her so.

There's angels that surround us all,
Most unaware to man,
But yet, protect us every hour,
Our spirits in demand.

Now, Heidi Jo herself could be
A pretty angel, bright.
She smiles just like the angels do,
"Tis quite a lovely sight.

I paused to view another tier
Inside of Heidi Jo,
And as I touched the quivering tier,
My spirit trembled So.

This tier shared words of deep concern
And worry, for this soul.
It tried to coax her every hour,
To find a wholesome goal.

We trembled there together, so,
To see her path of shame.
What danger, in disguise of joy,
Has scorched her like a flame!

The mission of this quivering tier,
Is quite an awesome strain—
Convincing one, we love so dear,
She's walking toward great pain.

God's hand is in the midst of her,
My prayers are with her, too,
And all the lust inside of her
Does not know what to do.

Those evil—doers, in her life
Will flee one day, I know,
And spare the soul we pray so for,
And free my Heidi Jo.

Then, Heidi Jo, in all her joy,
Her smiles, to full refine,
Will walk a path so straight and pure,
The whole wide world will shine.

And with the glory of the Lord
Surrounding her free life,
This tier that quivers in her, so,
Will have no longer strife.

The very space around her life
Is joyous for us all.
You cannot look upon this lass,
Without a curtain call.

You have to see her once again,
Her smile attracts that way.
Her heart is like a whispering wind:
So gentle, on display.

And when the whispering wind dies down
And gentle tones are calm,
Then, through the eyes of Heidi Jo,
I see a peaceful psalm.

And in the psalm, there's words of love,
So sacred, as they flow:
For all the words come through the heart,
Of my sweet, Heidi Jo.

Yes, through the eyes of Heidi Jo,
There are many songs and smiles.
There are songs of love and smiles of hope
And joyous tiers, for miles.

Within her soul, deep down inside,
There stands a tier of songs.
It sings so sweet, in harmony—
It's there, where it belongs.

This tier of songs, so beautiful,
With tones so crystal clear,
Fulfills its mission constantly—
I crave this singing tier.

If I could visit all the tiers
That dwell in Heidi Jo,
And linger there throughout my life,
Such tender joys would flow.

Her precious smile could wake the sun
On any cloudy day.
Yes, Heidi Jo is my great joy,
She's in my heart to stay.

But, if my heart, in God's command,
Should cease to beat no more,
Then, in my soul, I'd take her joy
With me, through Heaven's door.

And with this joy, to cloak my soul,
Eternal, it would be,
What gifts I'd have to share above,
Throughout eternity!

And if the joy that I would share,
Would dwindle from demand,
I'd have my Heidi Jo up there,
To let me hold her hand.

Her touch would charge my soul again,
With joy beyond compare,
And then, I'd have a thousand years
Of joy, again, to share.

The touch, the joy, of Heidi Jo,
Is always soft and kind,
And if her kindness goes awry,
I'll tell you what she'd find...

She'd reach way down inside of her,
And find a smile for you—
That's just the way of Heidi Jo,
Her spirit is so true.

And when the sad times take their toll
Upon her heart, so sweet,
She, too, needs strength from God above,
To keep her from defeat.

My prayers are with my Heidi Jo,
I know God hears them all.
My heart, in hand, is hers alone,
None other meets the call.

I give to Heidi Jo, my heart,
I give to her my best,
I give to God, for Heidi Jo,
A prayer with deep request...

I pray that Heidi Jo will find
The path that leads to home,
So she'll not linger in the sand,
And wander there, alone.

Her quest for joy has led her on
To paths unfit to tread.
My soul has mourned for Heidi Jo—
My heart has wept and bled.

The clock ticks on for Heidi Jo,
The time is almost gone.
I pray she'll join the journey up,
Before that early morn

When God, Himself, will send His Son,
To take the harvest home.
She hesitates on this great quest,
To linger here and roam.

Pull from these tiers, within your soul,
And look to God above.
Please, Heidi Jo, forsake this life,
And come with those you love.

God will not e'er forsake her heart,
She knows He's always there,
And deep within those tiers of hers,
She knows, there dwells a prayer.

It's been sometime since I have seen,
The tiers of Heidi Jo.
I ache to visit there again,
I pray, one day, I'll go.

Oh, how my heart longs for the tiers,
I dearly miss, so much.
I pray, one day, I'll find again,
Her sweet and tender touch.

And when I find it, I will know,
Her smile, her heart—felt tears,
And through her eyes, I'll see the joy
Of all those precious tiers.

And in the journey to the tiers,
My heart will fill once more,
With overwhelming joy and love,
From one I knew before.

I only wish that I could tell
In human words, to all,
What I have seen in Heidi Jo
Through eyes without a flaw.

I could have spent a life time there,
Just looking through her eyes,
And into all the tiers of time
Of one with no disguise.

Most vivid is a journey to
The tier of great delight,
That stands beside the tier of joy,
In Heidi Jo—so bright.

It gives great pleasure to her soul
When time recalls its need,
Look for the good times, Heidi Jo,
And use this tier, indeed.

Another tier in Heidi Jo,
I simply can't forget,
Is that tall tier of loneliness,
Which trembles with regret,

It does not want to be inside
of Heidi Jo's sweet heart,
But has no choice, but to remain
"Till heartaches all depart.

I pray that Heidi Jo will give
This tier another choice,
And lift her eyes to Heaven above
And let God hear her voice.

I know my Heidi Jo is strong,
I know her heart is true,
Things just deceive her so, sometimes,
But she'll be pulling through.

The many smiles of Heidi Jo,
Are all a bright display.
They're sure a precious gift of God,
That light up every day.

The smiles of wonder, shining bright;
The smiles of gracious peace;
The smile of joy; the smile of hope—
Her smiles just will not cease.

And in my heart, the smiles of one
That I hold close and dear,
Sings to my soul in lovely voice,
I hear her smile so clear.

This time on earth is nearly gone
And Heidi Jo smiles on;
I know she'll take those smiles along,
When Heaven's finally won,

And there in Heaven, with those smiles,
The angels too, will say,
"Thank God on high for Heidi Jo"—
Will be a lovely day.

Now all the smiles that come from her
Dwell in her heart, alone.
She smiles the one just right for you,
Her joy flows from God's throne.

And from God's throne, flows more than joy—
There flows eternal life.
For Heidi Jo it puts aside,
Her daily toil and strife.

I pray one day she'll understand,
The many tiers inside,
That whisper to her every day
Cross rivers, deep and wide.

The tier of flowing water, soft,
That flows in Heidi Jo,
Is such a comfort to her soul
When she is feeling low.

My Heidi Jo is human, too,
To that, I can attest.
She has the low times in her life,
But always does her best.

The flowing water from this tier,
A flowing, living well—
Is God's great hand of love and care,
Her savior there, doth dwell.

This river running in her soul,
Is life for Heidi Jo.
The tier is bubbling o'er with love,
To hold her when she's low.

I know the lonely tier I've seen
In my sweet Heidi Jo,
Makes tears fall from her lovely eyes—
The eyes where rivers flow.

Oh, tier of rivers, running free,
Flow on in one so swell,
And give the soul of Heidi Jo,
Drink from Your living well.

And with Your gorgeous water fall,
Send comfort to her heart,
And give her peace from this great tier,
Lest all her joy, depart.

When pain suppresses Heidi Jo,
Her smile is there, but weak,
Yet when the tier of water flows,
The joy is hers to seek.

So many cups of tender joy,
Have overflowed with love;
Love through the heart of Heidi Jo,
As gentle as a dove.

She's shared those cups of joy with me,
So often o'er the years.
And now, I crave those happy times
With laughter and the cheers.

The memories of yesterday,
The vision of her nears—
And through her lonely, lovely eyes,
She whispers cups of tears.

She tried to tell me of the pain
And trouble she's been through,
But she didn't have to say a word,
My heart already knew.

I cannot only see the hurt:
I feel her pain inside.
I see the tears the—cup of tears —
The silver tears of pride.

Don't be ashamed, my Heidi Jo,
Don't be afraid to cry;
It's just God's way to purge your soul,
And lift your sunlight high.

Walk on—live life, sweet Heidi Jo,
But live it wholesomely,
And with your heart, let all those smiles
Shine to eternity.

As you walk through life's hardest times,
And find the going rough,
Reach down inside you, Heidi Jo,
It's there, you have enough.

I've truly seen a tier so bold
Stand firm in Heidi Jo.
This tier of boldness makes her strong
And gives her faith to grow.

Your life, my lass, like all on earth,
Cannot be free of woe.
God tries us all in His own way—
Be faithful, Heidi Jo.

Use all the good tiers in your soul,
Reject those clouded tiers.
And use your heart, sweet Heidi Jo,
To help you through the years.

Don't hurt the ones who love you so,
Tread well, as life allows.
Be very careful, Heidi Jo,
And use your tier of smiles.

Now some tiers whispered quietly,
And some tiers sang aloud.
Some tiers just trembled every hour
And some, a darkened cloud.

I saw a tier of warfare,
Inside of Heidi Jo.
It beckoned me to join it there,
My spirit would not go.

I felt the terrible pangs of war,
I prayed to God above,
To send His force to Heidi Jo,
And fight for one we love.

To conquer in her very soul,
This tier of dreadful war,
So Heidi Jo can rid this space
Of Satan's painful lure.

God will not burden Heidi Jo
With more than she more can bear.
He sees the tender tears that drop,
He knows her every care.

God knows the heart of Heidi Jo,
He knows each tier within.
And He will not abandon her,
He knows how hard life's been.

God knows how sensitive she is:
So tender, yet, so bold—
No man dare even dream about
The wonder I behold.

So precious are the pathways there,
Beneath her lovely eyes.
The beauty of her gracious heart,
So begs my soul to rise.

When all the light in Heidi Jo,
Beams out into my heart,
Then stands my soul, just like a king,
For my dear queen's impart.

And when she shares with me her joy
And both our hearts are full,
Then stardust sparkles through her eyes,
Just like a precious jewel.

And there I see, but once again,
Through eyes just God could make,
More tiers of time of Heidi Jo—
The trek is mine to take.

Some tiers I love to visit oft',
Some tiers just make me weep,
Some tiers just make me tremble so,
And others hurt me deep.

A tier of darkness stood in wait,
To steal my Heidi Jo,
And take her soul to death below
Where no one wants to go.

Don't yield your life to men of horror,
Please, Heidi Jo, I pray.
It makes the tier of darkness grow,
To blacken out your day.

Come out of darkness Heidi Jo,
Put down those whims of sin,
And lift your heart to God, on high,
Let His true light come in.

Don't let this dreadful tier, so dark,
Deceive your tender heart.
You have the faith to step aside
And let this tier depart.

I saw a tier in Heidi Jo,
Confused at what to do.
This tier spent time—persistent time—
To make her heart untrue.

It tried to make her change her mind,
And turn from what is right.
The tier kept working on her mind,
Determined on a fight.

This tier, in darkness, stood prepared,
To battle Heidi Jo—
To take control of her own soul,
And drag it far below.

But, little did this dark tier know,
That in my Heidi Jo,
There stood a tier of prayer up front,
To battle wicked foe.

Now when confusion strikes her so,
To squeeze her tender heart,
The tier of prayer is there for her—
Her soul will not depart.

The tier of prayer is those who pray
For Heidi Jo each day.
It keeps her safe and keeps her sure
And lifts her sky of gray.

For Heidi Jo, the struggle's great,
Confusion strikes her oft',
But when the tier of prayer stands firm,
Her life becomes so soft.

Her smile glows bright upon her face,
The demon flees away,
And Heidi Jo is free again;
Prayer always works that way.

The most important tier of all
That dwell in Heidi Jo,
Is the marvelous tier of prayer—
Its wonders overflow.

When darkness rises in her life,
And trouble grips her hard,
The tier of prayer wells up in her,
And stands a constant guard.

The tier of prayer protects her heart
And pulls her through the toil.
For Heidi Jo, it's one more day,
While tiers of darkness quarrel.

Now when the battles fully rage,
And thunder like a storm,
She feels no pain, she sees no wrong,
Her heart is all but warm.

My Heidi Jo has been deceived
By those she thought would care.
They're only friends to Satan's schemes,
Now darkness doth she bear.

Oh, Lord, don't let us lose this soul
That we need up above.
Reach down and hold my Heidi Jo
In Your great arms of love.

Please, wake her heart, so she may see
The pathway of her choice,
And let her see, the light of life
To hear the Savior's voice.

Rescue her soul, her heart, her mind,
And set her body free.
Protect this precious lass we love,
And pave her path with glee.

I know that lovely spirit dwells
Inside of Heidi Jo.
I've seen it many, many times,
Its light, so much aglow.

I know she has the will to live
A life more free and sure,
But blindness holds her like a charm
To keep her heart impure.

I pray to God, for Heidi Jo,
Each hour, each day, each night.
I know my God will lift, again,
That lovely inner light.

And when that light comes through her eyes.
She'll there, again, so thrive.
With gracious beauty all around,
She'll know our God's alive.

I know my Heidi Jo has will
Within her heart and soul,
To shun the wicked from her life,
And keep what's pure and whole.

She needs the strength from God above,
I pray, He'll give it her—
To flee this deadly game she plays,
That makes within a blur.

Lord, place Thy steps of faith before
The feet of Heidi Jo,
So she may step up to Your love,
From games she plays below.

Give her light again, I pray
And let her smile shine bright,
So all the evil tricking her,
Will make a speedy flight.

How can I live without her smile,
How can I here remain,
To walk my road in loneliness,
With naught, but tears and pain?

Would be a bitter thought in life,
To lose my Heidi Jo.
The time would be so dark and bleak,
My heart would hang so low.

My spirit longs to see again,
Those precious, lovely eyes
That take me to the tiers of time;
They're full of much surprise.

Each time I journey through her soul
And view those awesome tiers,
I find a new tier in her time—
Maturity, o'er the years.

How pleasant can her spirit be!
How graceful is her heart!
I see her beauty constantly,
From me, it can't depart.

Her tiers of time are hid within
This burning heart of mine.
No man dare take these tiers away—
God shields this christened vine.

To me alone God shows the path
Of tiers in Heidi Jo,
And as unworthy as I feel,
My heart still wants to go.

If I could live upon this earth
Another thousand years,
The paths I share with Heidi Jo
Would still bring joy and tears.

And now, her life has been unveiled
Before my spirit's eyes,
And what I've seen, I can't explain,
I only know she thrives—

She thrives on love from God above,
His hand is ever near.
Our God protects my Heidi Jo,
He knows her soul is dear.

And to her heart, He gives to her,
A blessing of her own.
It's all for her, from God on high
And all to her alone.

God loves her in a special way—
A way I can not know.
I only know my God and I,
Love dearly Heidi Jo.

And knowing all the love I hold
Inside my craving heart,
Makes me so anxious every day,
My mind could come apart.

And if my mind should burst with love,
My heart would open wide,
To show in part, to Heidi Jo,
What lies so deep inside.

And when she'd see the beauty there,
Within the depths of love,
I wonder if she'd understand
Such love, from God above?

The tier of understanding in
The heart of Heidi Jo,
Will speak to her of love so true
And surely let her know.

No greater love exists in time,
Than that which God bestows,
And this pure love is what I see
Inside of Heidi Jo.

Now, by the grace of God it be,
That from her soul I share
The tiers that take my breath away
And cause my heart to care.

I have not known such tenderness,
Nor have I known such love,
As what I've found in Heidi Jo—
A gift from God above.

I've never seen, in any heart,
Such human beauty flow,
Until I looked in through the eyes
Of lovely Heidi Jo.

No man alive can understand
The love of God on high,
Who freely shares with all of us,
From paths beyond the sky.

This kind of love is what I've seen
Inside of Heidi Jo.
"Tis why I know the hand of God
So Masters o'er her soul.

And from the pathways far beyond
The sky above us all,
God Masters more in Heidi Jo,
Than I could e'er recall.

He Masters all her tiers of time,
So many, I can't count
And to her heart He gives to her,
Much joy, of great amount.

The memories now of Heidi Jo
Still linger in my heart,
And speak to me most every day,
In time we spend apart.

The memories cannot fade away,
Her shadow is too bright;
My spirit craves her every hour
An everlasting light.

This precious lass of long ago
Seems centuries now, gone by—
Will never leave my banks of thought—
Eternal, though I die.

And if I die before my time,
This wretched life, lie still—
My Heidi Jo will still be here,
To light the world at will.

The light will shine from her great smile
And glow from her bright eyes—
The world will know it's Heidi Jo,
When all her beauties rise.

Not only do I crave the love
That dwells within her tiers,
From deep beyond her lovely eyes,
So precious o'er the years;

But crave I, for those paths of peace,
That map my Heidi Jo
With prints of smiles and tones of grace—
Where brooks of waters flow.

Those peaceful paths, beneath her eyes,
A very cunning treat,
And all the beauty in her soul,
Makes Heidi Jo complete.

If I go back to visit her
And walk those paths again,
I pray, I'll find the Heidi Jo
That once lived down the lane.

That precious lass, the beaming smile,
The lovely eyes, so bright.
And will I find her heart the same,
To fill me with delight?

I pray, that time has not pulled down,
The tiers of Heidi Jo,
Nor taken from her all the smiles,
That still, my heart doth know.

From Irish pilgrims long ago,
To now my Heidi Jo—
My heart still bleeds, my tears still flow,
Still love my Heidi Jo…

My precious Heidi Jo.